Safety for Kids

Equipping Children to Discern Danger

Julie Lowe

New Growth Press
newgrowthpress.com

New Growth Press, Greensboro, NC 27401
newgrowthpress.com

Cover Design: Dan Stelzer
Interior Typesetting and Ebook: Lisa Parnell, lparnellbookservices.com

ISBN: 978-1-64507-534-9 (print)
ISBN: 978-1-64507-535-6 (ebook)

Library of Congress Cataloging-in-Publication Data on file

Printed in the USA

29 28 27 26 25   2 3 4 5 6

It can take less than an hour of watching the local news to notice the dangers that our children confront every day in our world. Here are just some of the common risks that our children might encounter:

- Rising rates of youth depression, suicide, and anxiety[1]
- Marijuana and drug use becoming more common place
- Bullying and cyberbullying increasing with technology[2]
- Young children being exposed to pornography, sexting, and solicitation[3]
- Compounding issues related to sexual activity, orientation, and identity
- Internet addiction
- A growing culture of violence, objectification, and desensitization to the mistreatment of others
- Physical abuse, sexual abuse, date rape, and trafficking of young people
- School shootings, teens encouraging other teens to commit self-harm, and dangerous viral social media challenges
- Sextortion—a rising problem that targets young people

The Danger Also Lies Within

When we consider all the dangers our children might face, it can be tempting to think that the best way to protect our children is to never let them out of our sight. But even if this was practical (and it's not), would they be safe then? The Bible teaches us that there are not only dangers outside of us, there is danger within.

You can and should maintain a close watch on your children. You can and should monitor their activities and try to shelter them from harm. But you will find that the danger your children face cannot always be kept at bay. We must equip them to function wisely in the world and to know good from evil. Good parenting is not simply about putting up boundaries and high walls—protecting our children from the external dangers of this world. Wise parenting also helps children understand that there is danger from within. Sin resides in the heart and is not easily visible. Every person—loved ones, trusted friends and acquaintances, respectable individuals with whom we live and work—is capable of being led astray into destructive choices. This includes your own children.

Aleksandr Solzhenitsyn, in *The Gulag Archipelago*, says it like this: "The line separating good and evil passes not through states, nor between classes, nor between political parties either—but right through every human heart—and through all human hearts."[4]

Jesus tells us,

> "For from within, out of the heart of man, come evil thoughts, sexual immorality, theft, murder, adultery, coveting, wickedness, deceit, sensuality, envy, slander, pride, foolishness." (Mark 7:21–22)

Yes, each of us is vulnerable to evil happening *to* us, but we are also each capable of allowing it to take root *in* us. Our children need to be taught to guard their hearts, for it is the wellspring of life (Proverbs 4:23). James reminds us about the slippery slope of giving in to sinful desires: "Desire when it has conceived gives birth to sin, and sin when it is fully grown brings forth death" (James 1:15). We will fail our children if we only shelter them from the external perils of this world and do not foster in them a conviction that they must guard themselves from evil.

We can try to keep evil far from us, but we will fail because of the pervasive nature of sin and evil. Your children will be tempted by their own wrong desires. Just like you, they will sometimes fall. They will sometimes go in the wrong direction. But this is the very issue that the gospel of Jesus Christ addresses. Jesus died on a cruel cross because we are all sinners. On that cross, all our sins were forgiven—the sins of parents and children alike. Isaiah 53:6 says: "All we like sheep have gone astray; we have turned—every one—to his own way; and the Lord has laid on him the iniquity of us all." We have been rescued from ourselves—and continue to be. We and our families have been given the Spirit as a Helper and Comforter who transforms hearts and minds—places that no one else can go.

Our ultimate safety and our children's ultimate safety will be found in trusting a faithful Father, who has rescued us and continues to rescue us. Remember the good news you have to share with your children that Jesus Christ came to save sinners (1 Timothy 1:15). Then together you can remember that "he who is in you is greater than he who is in the world" (1 John 4:4).

Our children's greatest defense against the evil of this world is to know God and his ways. Then they will know the straight path to take and will be able to recognize the crooked path and avoid it. We should have no greater joy than that our children walk in truth (3 John 1:4). As a parent, do not grow weary in discipling your children. The Lord and his Spirit will be your help. Take encouragement for your journey from 2 Corinthians 9:8: "God is able to make all grace abound to you, so that having all sufficiency in all things at all times, you may abound in every good work."

Worry and Denial Are *Not* Safety Skills

> "And which of you by being anxious can add a single hour to his span of life?" (Matthew 6:27)

When it comes to addressing safety issues regarding our children, there are many common struggles parents face. Instead of facing reality head-on with an appropriate dose of both realism and faith, it is easy to veer off course in the diverging directions of either fear or denial. Neither response will enable you to make healthy decisions or appropriately equip your children for the challenges they will face. Neither response will enable you to grow in love and dependence on the Lord or help your child to do so. Let's dig into each struggle and see the better way Christ offers us.

Worry

Parents worry about germs, cancer, choking, kidnapping, drugs and alcohol, school performance and academics, and many other things—the list is endless. But worrying will not keep our kids safe. Our anxiety does nothing but take up time and mental energy.

We might think that if we put enough focused concern into all the possible dangers our children might face, we can will them out of existence. Our hope is that such hyper attention will produce some type of benefit. But what worry actually does is fill our minds with all the what-ifs and our own insecurities and fears of the future. It puts us in a state of perpetual fear and distracts us from living in the present and perceiving what is going on right in front of us. It hinders wisdom and discernment. To our anxious mind, everything feels like a threat, and this blurs our ability to see genuine threats clearly. We become unable to tell what is truly a danger and what is harmless.

Worry is crippling to both a parent and a child's sense of safety and stability. A parent who chronically worries will most likely raise a child who worries. Children who worry are not adept at handling challenges; rather, they struggle to take risks, try new things, and interact with people. Our worrying does not prevent harm; it *causes* harm to our children.

It is not by accident that Scripture says, "Fear not" over 365 times. The Bible is not implying that danger does not exist. Nor is it implying you will never have hard things happen to you or your children. Actually the Bible tells us to not be surprised by trials and tribulation, by suffering and evil—those things do exist (John 16:33; James 1:2–8; 1 Peter 4:12).

Worry sees all of the threats around us and tells us that God must not be present or in control—therefore, I feel like I have to figure out how to keep my children safe. But in the midst of trouble, God reminds us again and again that he is our refuge and "a very present help in trouble" (Psalm 46:1–3). Worry says, "I must figure out and control my world." Faith says, "God is in control and will equip me (or my child) with wisdom for the moment."

There will be plenty to fear in this world, but we cannot be ruled by it. As believers, we know there is a God who is sovereign over all. He is our help and a sure comfort in the hard places and times. Joshua 1:9 reminds us, "Have not I commanded you? Be strong and courageous. Do not be frightened, and do not be dismayed, for the LORD your God is with you wherever you go." In any difficult situation, we are called to trust God and to take steps of faith and courage. In the face of all the dangers our children might be exposed to, we trust God to be with us and to help us be wise, practice discernment, and do what we can to guard our families. Then we put our hope in him.

Denial

When faced with the threats our children may be exposed to, some parents choose denial. They take pride in not struggling with worry as other parents do. They occasionally look out the window while their young children play outside with their neighbor friend. The kids are jumping off rocks, running in and out of the houses, and climbing trees in the woods. The parents are confident that their children are happy and safe.

However, they might be oblivious to the older teenager who is also watching the kids play from his window. This teen struggles with pornography and has begun looking for ways to act out the sexual fantasies he has been watching. He sees his little brother playing with neighborhood kids, watches them running in and out of the house past him. He considers ways to entice one of the children into his room, the bathroom, or the basement while the other kids are distracted. He plans to bribe them with a movie or video game and isolate them so he can molest them.

Perhaps if someone were to tell you that such a possibility exists, you'd brush them off, call them an alarmist, or shake your head in disbelief. Denial ignores possibilities and refuses to accept that they could happen in their neighborhood, community, home, or family. Denial minimizes and explains away genuine concerns or red flags.

In a desire to avoid discomfort, or perhaps because we have no idea how to approach such matters, we tell ourselves that our children could never be sexually abused. We assure ourselves that we can keep our kids safe, that we know our neighbors and friends. Or perhaps we choose to believe we protect our kids by keeping them at home where evil cannot touch them. But we may be unaware that as they sit leisurely on the couch, they might be online with an older teen or adult who is sending them graphic pornography.

Denial suppresses concern; it ignores our instinct that something could be amiss. Because we want to be free from worry and fear, we close our minds (and our eyes) to the possibility of danger. We might feel concern about the way someone watches our child, but brush it off because we do not want to be skeptical of others. We feel uncomfortable that our children are in the basement unsupervised for a long period of time, but rather than check in on them, we tell ourselves it is silly to be distrustful.

Denial is an act of seeing sensing that something is wrong but refusing to face it. It is sometimes an intangible feeling or observation we cannot articulate. It points to a concern, yet we ignore or reject it. Denial lulls us into a false sense of comfort.

That perspective can lead to serious tragedy and a wealth of regret. It is always wise to notice when something seems amiss. Stopping to evaluate what you are observing will only make you more confident and competent at keeping your children safe.

The Need to Equip Our Kids

For over twenty years I have worked with churches, ministries, and families when the children under their care experienced abuse and mistreatment. I have met with many parents who ask heart-wrenching questions. They wonder how their child could have gotten caught up in online bullying, sexting, pornography, or grooming by a pedophile.

Parents and caregivers whose children have been victimized or hurt in some way struggle to understand how such grievous wrongs occurred. Was there something they could have done to prevent it? Did they miss warning signs? Are they responsible for their child's struggles? It is distressing to evaluate in hindsight.

Those questions are then followed up with: What can we do now? How can we help our child now? How can we prevent this in the future? The alarming statistics related to child sexual abuse, online predation, severe bullying by peers, and more leads thoughtful parents to ask: How do we protect children from such things? How do we proactively put in place safeguards to protect our children from danger?

God calls parents to protect and equip their children, who are born weak and vulnerable. You can apply biblical principles that result in commonsense, practical strategies that will help to safeguard your children so they can thrive.

Doing this begins with acknowledging that we live in a broken, fallen world. There is danger and evil, sickness and disease, corruption, deception, and temptation. We cannot live in this world without being touched by it, and our children will be touched by it too.

Consider these verses:

> We know that we are from God, and the whole world lies in the power of the evil one. (1 John 5:19)

> Evil people and imposters will go on from bad to worse, deceiving and being deceived. (2 Timothy 3:13)

Proverbs warns against "a troublemaker and a villain, who goes about with a corrupt mouth, who winks maliciously with his eye, signals with his feet and motions with his fingers, who plots evil with deceit in his heart" (Proverbs 6:12–14 NIV).

Dangerous people prey upon the weak and naive. Evil is cunning; it deceives and entices. It promises pleasure but delivers brokenness. Evil is both done to us and seduces us from within. Accepting this reality means that we must raise children who can navigate and respond to potential dangers.

Scripture is full of wisdom on how to respond to evil. In Matthew 10:16 Jesus tells us, "Behold, I am sending you out as sheep in the midst of wolves, so be wise as serpents and innocent as doves." Proverbs states, "The prudent sees danger and hides himself, but the simple go on and suffer for it" (27:12), and "One who is wise is cautious and turns away from evil, but a fool is reckless and careless" (14:16).

Wise People See the Potential for Danger and Take Care

The Bible teaches us that wise people see the potential for danger and take measures to protect themselves. Wise people are cautious and discerning and turn from evil. Those who do not act wisely are called simple and foolish, and they suffer for it. Clearly, nothing good comes from being unaware of the danger that exists in our world. Too often parents are unwilling to face the realities of the perils that exist in the world around us, and therefore conceal such realities from their children. But if we only shelter our children and do not equip them to act in wisdom, we inadvertently raise naive, simple children who do not know how to make sense of evil or how to wisely navigate it.

We teach our children to navigate this world by giving them the ability to discern good from evil and right from wrong. Our culture is pressing in on our children, indoctrinating them with false views of romance and love, morality and truth, sexuality and identity. Our world calls intolerant what is good and holy and calls good what God calls wicked. Isaiah 5:20 says, "Woe to those who call evil good and good evil, who put darkness for light and light for darkness, who put bitter for sweet and sweet for bitter!"

Keeping our children safe means teaching them God's ways—how he created us to follow him. Safety is built on the foundation of discerning right from wrong. Our children cannot safely navigate this world without the ability to distinguish good from evil. As a parent, my ultimate goal for my children is not to keep them safe (though it is *a* goal); rather, it is to have them know the ways of God and walk in truth. Walking by faith and knowing good from evil will be their shield, and I believe that safety skills are the fruit of teaching our children the ways of the Lord.

Teaching our children the difference between good and evil will produce wisdom and discernment in them. Wisdom and discernment are what I hope you (and your children) learn. Consider this verse: "Solid food is for the mature, for those who have their powers of discernment trained by constant practice to distinguish good from evil" (Hebrews 5:14). Notice that the mature have "*powers of discernment* trained by *constant practice* to *distinguish good from evil.*"

Discussing with our children (in an age-appropriate way) the dangers they might encounter helps us to understand how we can begin equipping both ourselves and them for taking appropriate protective measures. Equipping our children means naming the darkness that exists and teaching them how to avoid it and how to respond to it if it finds them. Understanding these things protects our young people from the temptations that exist and the entanglements of destructive choices.

Philippians 1:9–10 affirms this goal:

> It is my prayer that your love may abound more and more, with knowledge and all discernment,

> so that you may approve what is excellent, and so be pure and blameless for the day of Christ.

We are to commit ourselves to train, disciple, and equip our kids so that they have the myriad tools they need to wisely navigate this world while walking in fellowship with the Lord.

Knowing good from evil, right from wrong is primary; safety skills are secondary. Safety skills are a fruit of parenting our children wisely. This is important to emphasize, because if we raise children who somehow have been shielded from the worst perils of this world but do not walk with the Lord, do not know right from wrong, or are unaware of the dangers that exist from within—we have failed them miserably.

Our Safety Rests in God's Hands

We must also teach our children that our safety ultimately rests in God's hands. Psalm 37:39–40 reminds us, "The salvation of the righteous is from the LORD; he is their stronghold in time of trouble. The LORD helps them and delivers them; he delivers them from the wicked and saves them, because they take refuge in him." Our ultimate hope is in a sovereign God who is our high tower, our very present help in trouble (Psalm 46:1; Proverbs 18:10). The psalmist writes, "Though I walk in the midst of trouble, you preserve my life; you stretch out your hand against the wrath of my enemies, and your right hand delivers me" (Psalm 138:7).

Psalm 23 is a profound reminder that we will walk through dark valleys, we will face enemies, and we will come face to face with evil, but he will be our Shepherd guiding us and walking with us in the difficult places. His presence is our comfort, our hope, and our very present help.

We must teach our kids to navigate a broken world, but at the end of the day, God is the one who watches over them. Teaching kids to be safe is not our highest call. It is nurturing a personal relationship with a loving heavenly Father who will be their guide, and safety will be a fruit of knowing him. As we explore Scripture, we will understand more deeply the call to be wise, to see danger and run from it (Proverbs 27:12), to have courage (Proverbs 28:1; 2 Chronicles 32:7–9), and to stand up for those who cannot stand up for themselves (Isaiah 1:17; Proverbs 31:8–9). We are not to be passive in our engagement with injustice, danger, mistreatment, and evil. We must respond to it, while resting in our ultimate Protector.

Ways to Establish Safeguards

The goal is to equip you and your children. Again, safety is the fruit of distinguishing good from evil, of discernment and wisdom, so we must be wise, discerning people. The Lord reassures us that he gives wisdom generously to those who ask (James 1:5). We are entreated to not be caught off guard by the entrapments and perils of this world. We are to do all we can to safeguard our homes, equip our children, and trust the One who is our refuge. When we do this, we are able to lay our heads down at night because the Lord is our safety (Psalm 4:8). Our heavenly Father is our true safeguard and we can trust him.

Technology

With the advent of social media and personal electronic devices, a world of new possibilities—carrying with it both blessings and dangers—has entered our children's lives. Children and teens are being given devices with little preparation on how to steward them. These shiny devices open up a world of entertainment and connectivity to our children. Unless precise parental controls have been activated, children and teenagers have access to a wide range of online games and apps. They can text and video chat with anyone they wish. They have access to video streaming services, social media, and a wealth of information via internet browsers, and all of it is at their fingertips. Parents must steward their children's technology use carefully. Don't be afraid to take charge of how and when your children use technology.

Here are some questions for you to consider:

- How much screen time should children be allowed per day (this includes all screens)?
- How will you monitor what they are watching on their screens?
- How will you help them evaluate what they are watching?

- How will you equip them to respond when they are not at home and friends are watching inappropriate content?
- How can you encourage and teach mature stewardship and accountability of technology?

Peers

As children get older, they begin to ask questions related to their worldview and identity, and they want to know if what they have been taught is true. Preteens and teens often struggle to accept that their parents have the best answers about relationships, identity, activities, and even questions of meaning and purpose. They are drawn to the most persistent voices in their lives—their peers—to help answer these questions. The desire to fit in and please others is dangerously strong. This means that it matters who gets a voice into their lives. What kinds of friends are they choosing? Who are they spending large amounts of time with? Proverb says, "Whoever walks with the wise becomes wise, but the companion of fools will suffer harm" (Proverbs 13:20).

Access to smart phones, social media, and the internet mean that peer influence presses in more and more; it also means that parents struggle more and more to have a voice in their children's lives. Most parents want to be intentionally influencing and shaping their child's character, but that requires a significant investment of time and thought.

Here are some questions for you to consider:

- How are you intentionally building a relationship with your child?
- Do you have specific times that you spend with each of your children?
- Does your family eat meals together?
- What other family traditions could you incorporate into your home?
- How can you proactively foster conversations about hard topics? It is far better to proactively and biblically shape the way they think about a subject than to wait until they have been exposed to the corruption and try to fix it.
- How can you teach them to pay attention to things that make them uncomfortable and to ask themselves why those things make them uncomfortable?

Culture

We live in a world that is distinctly self-oriented. Our kids are inundated with moral relativism that seeks to sweep them away with the current of their peers. It is the cultural air they breathe; it is the environment they are educated in; and it is the constant beat of the media drum.

These messages lead our kids to question what is right and good. The surrounding culture can easily shape their values, ideas regarding moral absolutes, relationships, romance, sexuality, identity, and decision-making. A secular culture will sway your children to embrace a worldview devoid of God, and they can quickly be swept away by the ideology and behaviors that go with it.

It is sobering how it only takes one generation to lose sight of God's ways. The need for parents to safeguard their children from empty philosophies is as great as ever. Judges 2:10 says, "All that generation also were gathered to their fathers. And there arose another generation after them who did not know the LORD or the work that he had done for Israel."

Here are some questions for you to consider:

- How am I teaching my children discernment—to distinguish right from wrong, good from evil, wise from unwise, what is permissible from what is profitable?
- How can I bring God's Word to them in age-appropriate and meaningful ways?
- Is going to church a priority for us?
- Consider how your schedule sets the priorities for your family. What does your schedule teach your child about what you value the most?
- How can you encourage your children to find wise, mature advisors?

Our Confidence

As parents, we care for our children, protect them, and equip them with the knowledge, discernment, and abilities they need to navigate hazards. Then we implore them to trust the Lord in their time of need.

But it is important to remember that although we would like to believe that by doing these things we can keep our children completely safe, that is not our guarantee. Our children are moral responders, and they will be facing many of the things mentioned in this book; they will have to make choices to discern what is wise and to do what is right.

What will you do if you find your child has been victimized, or been the one committing the victimization? What will you do when your child caves to temptation, peer pressure, or makes foolish and risky decisions?

As a parent, you will most likely experience a range of emotions: surprise, devastation, grief, anger, maybe even helplessness and despair. You might feel shame that propels you to judge or condemn your child. When your child's actions have heartbreaking repercussions for themselves, you, or the family, you will face a barrage of conflicting emotions and reactions. Be aware of the impact they have on you. You may be tempted to be hopeless or to give up. Perhaps you want to abandon your child or cut them off from you and the rest of your family. Maybe you are overcome with anxiety or fear for the future.

The truth is that, at some point, you are likely to experience the heartbreak and discouragement that comes with loving your children through their temptations, struggles, foolish choices, and suffering. We don't always have a choice in what we will face alongside our children, but we can go to God for the help we need to respond in faith and love. We cannot possibly know all that lies before us and before our children, but we can know who goes with us. Our confidence and trust must ultimately be in the Lord. He is a refuge and help in times of trouble, not only for us but also for our children (Psalm 46:1). He is our shield and defender, and he is our children's shield and defender (Psalm 18:2). God does not guarantee that we will not face trouble, but he does promise that he will be our strength in the midst of it.

We may grieve and struggle with the weight of consequences, but we do so with the faith that God is with us in our struggle. He has not abandoned our children or us. He specializes in bringing beauty out of ashes, and he is able to do good even in the hardest of situations (Isaiah 61:3).

When you are tempted to despair because of your child's struggles and choices, turn to God's Word and let him interpret your future and your child's future for you. The apostle Paul, in the midst of deep trouble, affirmed to his fellow Christians that

> God causes all things to work together for good to those who love God, to those who are called according to His purpose. . . . What then shall we say to these things? If God is for us, who is against us? He who did not spare His own Son, but delivered Him over for us all, how will He not also with Him freely give us all things? Who will bring charges against God's elect? God is the one who justifies; who is the one who condemns? Christ Jesus is He who died, but rather,

> was raised, who is at the right hand of God, who also intercedes for us. Who will separate us from the love of Christ? Will tribulation, or trouble, or persecution, or famine, or nakedness, or danger, or sword? (Romans 8:28, 31–35 NASB)

Remember that it is God who will redeem. That eternal perspective gives you the ability to remember what is true, and to tell the difference between what is momentary and what is eternal. It shapes what we do with our heartache and suffering and where our confidence will lie. Parenting our children will bring a multitude of joys and also heartbreak. Christian homes are not immune from the trials of this world. Hard things happen to believers and unbelievers alike. However, God's promise to us is that he will be our refuge when the world crashes around our family. Godly hope positions us in the center of God's will and reminds us that we live for something better than that which is temporary. It gives us a vision to live for what is eternal so that we can trust God with our children's sufferings, as well as our own.

Commit to trust in God at all times—even and especially in the most disheartening of circumstances. For you know that what others mean for evil, God intends for good (Genesis 50:20). Believe by faith that he who began a good work will be faithful to complete it in your child's life (Philippians 1:6).

David, who was familiar with danger from outside and from within, wrote, "In peace I will both lie down and sleep; for you alone, O Lord, make me dwell in safety" (Psalm 4:8). In closing, I want to remind you to dwell in the One who is your source of safety and your child's source of safety. He is your refuge and strength and, come what may, will always be your refuge and strength. The Lord will be your safeguard and he will be your children's safeguard.

For practical ways you can prepare your children to navigate dangers, please read *Safeguards: Shielding Our Homes and Equipping Our Kids* by Julie Lowe.

Endnotes

1. Matt Richtel, "'It's Life or Death': The Mental Health Crisis Among U.S. Teens," *The New York Times*, April 23, 2022, https://www.nytimes.com/2022/04/23/health/mental-health-crisis-teens.html.

2. Sameer Hinduja and Justin W. Patchin, "Cyberbullying: Identification, Prevention, and Response," Cyberbullying Research Center. Retrieved April 26, 2022, https://cyberbullying.org/Cyberbullying-Identification-Prevention-Response-2021.pdf.

3. Kimberly J. Mitchell, Lisa Jones, David Finkelhor, and Janis Wolak, "Trends in Unwanted Sexual Solicitations: Findings from the Youth Internet Safety Studies," Crimes Against Children Research Center, University of New Hampshire, February 2014, https://www.unh.edu/ccrc/sites/default/files/media/2022-02/trends-in-unwanted-sexual-solicitations.pdf.

4. Aleksandr Solzhenitsyn, *The Gulag Archipelago 1918–1956* (Harper and Row, 1974).